★★★ Football's ★★★
INCREDIBLE BULKS

★★★ Football's ★★★
INCREDIBLE BULKS

Nate Aaseng

Lerner Publications Company
Minneapolis

Front cover: William "The Refrigerator" Perry throws his weight around against Minnesota Viking guard Mark MacDonald.
Page 1: New York Giant fans celebrating a play-off win over the 49ers in 1985 relished the challenge of facing football's latest larger-than-life legend.
Page 2: Seeing that the quarterback has released the ball, Dave Butz (shown here playing for St. Louis) backs off. Kansas City center Jack Rudnay received no such consideration from Butz.

Copyright © 1987 by Lerner Publications Company

Library of Congress Cataloging-in-Publication Data

Aaseng, Nathan.
  Football's incredible bulks.

  (Sports talk)
  Summary: Brief biographies of ten star football
players noted for their massive size as well as
their outstanding athletic skills.
  1. Football players — United States — Biography —
Juvenile literature. 2. National Football League —
Biography — Juvenile literature. [1. Football players]
I. Title. II. Series.
GV939.A1A1658 1987   796.332'092'2 [B] [920]   87-2895
ISBN 0-8225-1532-6 (lib. bdg.)

Manufactured in the United States of America

1 2 3 4 5 6 7 8 9 10 96 95 94 93 92 91 90 89 88 87

★★★ Contents ★★★

They Blot Out the Sun   7

1   Les Bingaman:
Wide and Wonderful   17

2   Gene Lipscomb: Big Daddy   23

3   Roosevelt Grier: The Gentle Giant   29

4   Sherman Plunkett:
Namath's Wall of Protection   35

5   Roger Brown:
The Thanksgiving Day Terror   41

6   Ernie Ladd:
Football's Most Dangerous Man   47

7   Bubba Smith:
Legend Before His Time   53

8   Pete Johnson: The Backfield Bull   59

9   Dave Butz: The Invisible Giant   67

10   William Perry: The Refrigerator   73

With a little more meat on his bones, Pittsburgh Steeler tackle Joe Greene could have made the lineup for this book. Still, he could manhandle opponents such as the Dallas Cowboys (above).

They Blot Out the Sun

So you think the ultimate in power football is a brute like Larry Csonka or John Riggins roaring into a stacked goal-line defense like a runaway 18-wheeler? Sorry, but we're looking for a fullback with a little more meat on his bones. You say that massive blockers such as Art Shell and John Hannah blot out the sun when they lumber onto the field? Well, I'm afraid we don't have room on the team for teeny tummies like them. Would you like to assemble an intimidating defensive wall made up of such massive brutes as "Mean" Joe Greene, Dan Hampton, and Ed "Too Tall" Jones? While that may sound like a coach's dream, those guys are just too small to rate a chapter in this book. We're talking *big*—as in mountainous, earth-shaking sauropods; people who could clean out your refrigerator quicker than a horde of locusts; athletes whose greatest dread throughout a brutal pro football training camp is stepping on a scale.

Part of pro football's appeal is the sight of giants engaging in a struggle of raw power. For the average person, trying to block or tackle some of the world's largest athletes would be like trying to knock down a Clydesdale. But every so often, a man of truly monstrous proportions enters the league—a man so enormous even 260-pound linemen will not make a move on the field without first checking the whereabouts of this terror.

But just pure size and strength doesn't count for much in pro football. Nearly every year, there is a story about a high school team that, despite having linemen who average over 300 pounds, still loses more games than it wins. Dozens of 300-pounders have been discarded by the pros because they didn't have the speed, the agility, and the coordination needed to put their size to use. The players highlighted in this book have been good ballplayers because they were good athletes, and their size made them dangerous ballplayers. When they closed in on an opponent, one sometimes wondered if they were going to simply defeat him or instead swallow him whole. Mass times speed equals a lot of damage!

Until the recent emergence of William "The Refrigerator" Perry as a media darling, pro football had been a difficult place for these mega-maulers. Because they seemed larger than life, fans and coaches often expected superhuman performances from them. If they didn't dominate a game from the opening play to the end, people wanted to know what was wrong with them. Instead of being accepted as real persons, these huge men sometimes found themselves stereotyped as either illiterate cavemen or fat, jolly Santa Clauses. They seemed so indestructible that fans forgot they, like anyone else, were susceptible to injuries, both physical and emotional. Worst of all, the size that appeared to be such an advantage was often their worst disadvantage. Many large players were simply overweight, struggling with the frustration of trying to get rid of pounds so they could function as efficiently as their lighter teammates.

In this book, a wide-angle lens has been focused on 10 players in National Football League (NFL) history whose combination of size, speed, and skill made them almost legendary. But when you discuss huge football players, it can be like talking about the nation's budget: it's hard to relate to 700 billion dollars or 300 pounds. To get a perspective on how big we're thinking, let's ease into the subject with a brief look at some of the giants who were too small to qualify for this book but who deserve honorable mention.

Like people in general, pro football players in the 1920s were not as large as they are now. Relatively speaking, however, Wilbur "Fats" Henry was The Refrigerator of his time. Born in Mansfield, Ohio, in 1897, Henry grew to a most unusual shape. At 5 feet, 10 inches and about 250 pounds, he looked nothing like an athlete. He didn't feel like one either. One opponent claimed that when you tried to block him, your head went in up to your neck. When Henry arrived for practice at Washington & Jefferson College in 1916, with his large belly much in prominence, his bug-eyed coach asked him what position he played. The coach nearly gagged when Henry claimed to be a running back and quickly convinced the new arrival he had better play in the line instead.

Despite the weight he carried, Henry was fast on his feet and could run up and down the field without getting winded. He lettered in four college sports, punted and kicked field goals as well as he played tackle, and showed an amazing knack for blocking kicks.

Wilbur Henry practices his punting back in the early days of Refrigeration.

Henry shot off the line so quickly he once snatched the ball from a punter and raced for a touchdown before the man even got his foot on the ball.

The NFL was just getting organized when Henry arrived in 1920, but he managed to bull his way into the record books by anchoring the line for the Canton Bulldogs during their 24-game unbeaten streak in 1922-23. Playing with Canton and later with the Pottsville Maroons, Fats Henry once won a game by kicking a 55-yard field goal. On another occasion, he blasted a 94-yard punt! Back in the days of the drop kick, Henry once compiled a record of 49 straight successful drop kicks. Opponents who tried to block him felt like they were bouncing off rubber, and they had no greater chance of rooting him out of his position than they did of removing the perpetual smile from his face during a game. As a result, Wilbur Henry has been named to virtually every NFL All-Decade team of the 1920s.

Players who were truly large by modern standards didn't begin making an impact on the game until the 1950s. On pro rosters, players' weights are often purposely fudged, and even today accurate figures are only guesses. But San Francisco may have been one of the first teams to experiment with giants.

They struck the jackpot with a pair of All-Pros, a rugged 265-pound defensive tackle named Leo Nomellini and Bob St. Clair, a 6-foot, 9-inch, 270-pound offensive tackle. Although the 49ers didn't win any championships during the giants' tenure, these two roughnecks made life miserable for opponents.

The Baltimore Colts also discovered that big was beautiful and rode their huge horses to ride to a pair of championships. With beefy Art Donovan, struggling to stay at 270 pounds during the season, teamed with "Big Daddy" Lipscomb in the defensive line and 275-pound perennial All-Pro tackle Jim Parker protecting quarterback John Unitas, the Colts won NFL titles in 1958 and 1959.

Few offensive tackles cared to tangle with Chicago Bear defensive end Doug Atkins, who stood 6 feet, 8 inches, weighed over 270 pounds, and harbored no sympathy for opponents. Atkins secured his side of the Bear line from 1955 to 1966, and his efforts were finally rewarded when the rest of the Bears matched his standards in their championship year of 1963.

When the passing game became the main offensive weapon in the 1960s and 1970s, coaches began looking for immovable blocks of pass-protecting granite rather than smaller, more nimble, run-blocking linemen. The most menacing of the bunch was Bob "The Boomer" Brown. A powerful 6-foot, 5-inch, 285-pound tackle from the University of Nebraska, Brown labored for mediocre Eagle teams before finishing championship years with the Rams and the Raiders. After being traded to Oakland in 1971, Boomer got his teammates' attention at the first practice by taking a shot at a goalpost and felling it with one block. St. Louis came up with 280-pound left tackle Ernie McMillan in the 1960s and topped that with All-Pro stalwart 290-pound right tackle Dan Dierdorf in the 1970s. The result was pleasant working conditions for Cardinal quarterbacks such as Jim Hart.

After a career of grunting and sweating in "the pit," tackle Dan Dierdorf (73) went on to become one of pro football's more articulate broadcasters.

San Diego's 290-pound tackle Russ Washington gave Charger quarterbacks such as Dan Fouts a decade of protection into the 1980s. Somehow Oakland's Art Shell was stuck under the shadow of smaller and more colorful teammates. Although he weighed nearly 290 pounds and owned a permanent spot on the All-Pro team, Shell could walk unrecognized down any street in the country.

The left tackle spot on the AFC's Pro Bowl team wasn't big enough for this pair of 78's. Fortunately, Art Snell (left) was ready to turn over his domination of the position just when Anthony Munoz (above) entered stardom.

Cincinnati's Anthony Munoz, 285 pounds of mobile aggressiveness, has carried on the tradition of the giant tackle.

A few mammoth blockers with exceptionally quick feet found homes as guards, where they used their bulk to

12

plow openings for running backs and protect quarterbacks. As if weighing 285 pounds wasn't enough, Ed White boasted bulging arms that earned him the title of arm-wrestling champion of the NFL. White threw his weight around for championship teams at Minnesota in the 1970s and later at San Diego. No offensive guard, however, hit harder than John "Hog" Hannah of New England. Since joining the NFL in 1973, the 275-pounder probably did more damage than any other offensive lineman of his time. In fact, after a week of practicing against Hannah, Patriot teammates who could still function looked forward to the relative peace and tranquility of game day!

On the other side of the line, the Kansas City Chiefs easily outmuscled rivals in acquiring beef in the 1960s and 1970s. At one time or another, the Chiefs dared opponents to move the ball against 6-foot, 7-inch, 285-pound Buck Buchanan; 6-foot, 7-inch, 290-pound Wilbur Young; and 6-foot, 8-inch, 275-pound John Matuszak. In an era when nose tackles were considered quaint souvenirs of the old college game, Buchanan would terrorize pro centers and guards by sliding over from his tackle spot and lining up nose-to-nose with them. The other Superchiefs didn't pan out as well, however, nor did the oversized gladiators trained by the Raiders to counter their archrivals. At 6 feet, 9 inches, and 290 pounds, Oakland's Ben Davidson lasted only a few years.

While leading the Steel Curtain defense that was largely responsible for Pittsburgh winning four Super Bowl titles, fire-breathing "Mean" Joe Greene

Patriot star John Hannah once said that because of his body, his occupational choices were limited to offensive guard or nightclub bouncer.

tipped the scales at about 275 pounds. Lining up at an angle between the center and the right guard, Greene led the charge that totally destroyed the Vikings in Super Bowl IX. During the same years, New England tried to disguise Sam Hunt as a linebacker. Although he was a solid tackler, Hunt's reign as the world's heaviest linebacker—approach-ing 280 pounds—was cut short by the increased emphasis on quicker line-backers to defend against the pass.

Finally, there was the original football appliance, defensive tackle Louie "The Refrigerator" Kelcher. Weighing about 280 pounds and still growing, Kelcher joined the San Diego Chargers in 1975. After several All-Pro seasons, including

Louie Kelcher treats himself to a quarterback, Seattle's Jim Zorn.

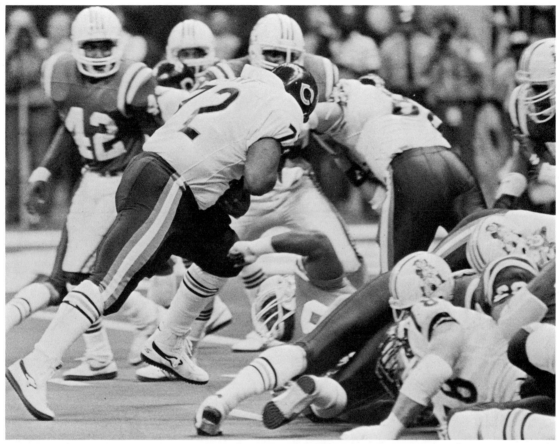

Blasting over for a score against the Patriots, The Fridge steals the spotlight from Walter Payton in Super Bowl XX.

a 1980 campaign in which he and his teammates recorded a league-high 60 sacks, Kelcher virtually ate himself out of a job. The Chargers dealt him to San Francisco in 1984 where, listed at 310 pounds, he saw spot duty in their championship season. Had the 49ers decided to spring their Refrigerator as a surprise blocking back in the Super Bowl against Miami, the Chicago Bears would have needed a new name for the man who suddenly brought fat back into style: William Perry.

Now that we've whetted your appetite for more bulk, let's bring on football's truly magnificent, mammoth manhandlers.

Les Bingaman did not need a press agent or a catchy nickname to attract the attention of opposing centers in the 1950s.

Les Bingaman

Wide and Wonderful

In the fashion business, they say that if you hold on to your outdated clothes long enough, they will eventually come back into style. National Football League fans of the 1980s who have been raving about William "The Refrigerator" Perry as the greatest use of fat since the invention of bacon would do well to remember this. Those with long football memories can point out that The Refrigerator is nothing new. A man with a build almost identical to his was thrilling fans and terrorizing opponents long before Perry was born.

Not far from the Windy City of Chicago, where Perry was launched to fame, prowled a Detroit Lion even bigger and bulkier than The Refrigerator. Although he was never swamped with commercial offers, never became a household name, or never even sported a descriptive nickname, Les Bingaman filled more space on a football field— and filled it better—than any other man of his time.

Born in 1926, in MacKenzie, Tennessee, Lester Bingaman was not always the food-inhaling giant one might have expected. Throughout his life, he rarely ate more than one large meal a day. Breakfast didn't appeal to him very much, and lunch generally consisted of several sandwiches. Although he had extremely wide feet (size 11EEE shoes), Bingaman did not reach mammoth proportions until after college. As a 265-pound middle guard at the University of Illinois, Bingaman made no All-American teams and played just well enough to attract the interest of the Detroit Lions.

Although his weight would be considered about average for a pro lineman of today, Bingaman was viewed as an oddity when he was drafted by the Lions in 1948. At that time, football was not a game for giants. Most pro teams included only one or two men over 240 pounds on their rosters, and even some of the lineman positions were manned by mere 200-pounders. Bingaman was considered unusual, and, once he started growing and throwing that weight around, the era of the "normal-sized" football player was over. The Lions were quite toothless in those days, and they had nothing to lose by experimenting with Bingaman, whose weight quickly grew past the 300-pound mark. Bingaman's extra heft made little difference at first as Detroit won only 2 of 12 games in his rookie season and posted losing years the next two.

A decision Bingaman made during training camp in 1951 tipped the scales in the Lions' favor, however. The 6-foot, 3-inch Bingaman reported to practice at a relatively trim 290 pounds. While shedding those pounds should have put Bingaman in better shape with more stamina and made him quicker on his feet, he instead felt he was being pushed around too much on the practice field. His solution was to buckle down to some serious eating and build himself back into an immovable block.

During the next five seasons, Les Bingaman took to the field weighing as much as 350 pounds—not counting his equipment—and he played as well as any lineman in the NFL. Some critics scoffed that Bingaman's only skill was to clog up the line of scrimmage and joked that he was one of the few people in the world who earned a living by standing still. But Les was much more than an immovable mass. Opponents credited him with being an intelligent player with good football instincts and surprising agility. Chicago Bears' Coach George Halas observed that Bingaman gave them more problems than any other lineman in the NFL. He admitted the only solution he could come up with was to stay away from Bingaman's area of the field.

But even that strategy didn't work very often. With Bingaman's 55-inch chest and 50-inch waist taking up so much room in the line, there wasn't a great deal of area left to work with. The Detroit Lions took advantage of this and constructed a unique defense. They placed Les in front of the offensive center as a middle guard and spread their other defenders wide to either side. So confident were the Lions in Bingaman's ability to control the middle of the line that they positioned their tackles and ends farther down the line where they could shut down end runs and off-tackle plays.

Big Les also freed the linebackers to

work the flanks. On most plays, the Lions relied on him so heavily that they didn't station a linebacker anywhere in his vicinity. Occasionally, a Lion opponent could take advantage of this empty spot by trapping Bingaman out of position and by springing a running back into the wide-open secondary. But most of the time, Les held his ground, fighting off two or three blockers at a time and plugging up the middle better than banana peels in a garbage disposal. The sheer effort of such pit-fighting caused Bingaman to lose about 20 pounds a game.

From 1951 to 1954, it was as difficult to move Les from the All-Pro ranks as it was to root him out of his defensive position. During each of those seasons, Detroit posted winning records, including NFL championships in 1952 and 1953. Typical of Bingaman's role in these successes was his performance in the 1953 title contest against the Cleveland Browns. On the second play of the game, Les pounced on a fumble that led to an early Detroit score. Although trapped out of position on a long Cleveland scoring run, he anchored an aroused defense that allowed the great Otto Graham only three completions in 16 attempts for a total of nine yards as the Lions eeked out a 17-16 win.

As increased television coverage brought to football fans the sight of this

It took Hall of Famer Otto Graham three tries before he found a way to get past the Bingaman-led Lions in an NFL championship game. Graham's Browns lost to the Lions in 1952 and 1953 before exploding for 56 points in 1954.

Bingaman's fumble recovery set up this Doak Walker touchdown plunge in the 1953 champion-ship game. (Walker is the man doubled over near the goal post.)

enormous man romping through enemy lines, Bingaman became one of the more popular players in the league, and he was sadly missed when he retired after the 1955 season. Even though he ushered in the era of the big lineman, it would be 30 years before the NFL saw a player as wide and as wonderful as Les Bingaman.

LES BINGAMAN: WIDE & WONDERFUL

Born: 1926 in MacKenzie, Tennessee

Size: 6 feet, 3 inches; 285-350 pounds

College: University of Illinois

Pro Draft: 1948; third round by Detroit Lions

All-Pro: 1951, 1952, 1953, 1954

Pro Bowl: 1952, 1954

Team Records:	YEAR	TEAM	WINS	LOSSES	TIES	POINTS	POINTS ALLOWED
	1948	Detroit	2	10	0	200	407
	1949	Detroit	4	8	0	237	259
	1950	Detroit	6	6	0	321	285
	1951	Detroit	7	4	1	336	259
	1952	Detroit	9	3	0	344	192
	1953	Detroit	10	2	0	271	205
	1954	Detroit	9	2	1	337	189

First-Place Finishes: 1952, 1953, 1954

NFL Titles: 1952, 1953

"Hey, little man! Where you going?" Big Daddy's famous greeting is about to be delivered enthusiastically to Los Angeles Ram running back Ron Walker (27).

★★★2★★★
Gene Lipscomb

Big Daddy

At 6 feet, 6 inches and 285 pounds, Big Daddy Lipscomb looked as if he could carry the world on his shoulders. Unfortunately, all too often he felt as if he were forced to do just that. On May 10, 1963, those shoulders finally dropped their load, ending the career and life of one of the most colorful giants the game of football has ever known.

People have said Eugene Lipscomb was never able to escape the fear that followed him since his birth in 1931 in Detroit, Michigan. Living in a slum, Eugene's father died shortly after his birth, and his mother was stabbed to death when Eugene was 11. With no brothers and sisters, Lipscomb had reason to be scared. Although he lived with a grandmother, he had to go to work at a young age to support himself. As a teenager, he worked the midnight-to-7 AM shift at a steel mill and

then headed straight to school. There he was laughed at because of his poor spelling and teased because of his size. With no proper supervision, Lipscomb ran into problems with the law and twice landed in jail for minor offenses. Although far larger than his classmates, he had good coordination and found an escape in basketball and football. But after it was discovered he had accepted money for playing with a softball team one summer, school sports were declared off-limits. It was little wonder that Gene finally quit school and left Detroit to join the U.S. Marines at age 18.

After watching Lipscomb pick up 40-pound cannon pieces with his fingers, a major knew this was the shot putter he wanted for the marine track team. With little training, Lipscomb found he could throw the shot with some of the best in the country. He also played football for the marines and showed enough promise for the Los Angeles Rams to sign him to a contract in 1953.

Lipscomb's few tastes of success were not enough to inject him with any confidence, however. Fearful of being cut, he would hit viciously and not always legally in practice. Frequently, his eagerness would get the best of him, and he would charge ahead without thinking, easily getting trapped out of position. Gene's poor, reckless play led to numerous fights with teammates and brought scorn from the veterans.

Although Lipscomb managed to make the team, he wasn't making any friends. Trying desperately to get the other Rams to like him, Lipscomb thought all he had to do to be a hero was to put his opponents out of the game. Before long, he earned the nickname "15-yard Daddy" in honor of all the personal foul penalities he earned with his cheap shots. Uneasy around this uncontrolled maniac —who once put himself out of action when he cut an artery punching through a car window—the Rams banished Gene to the bench. In 1956, they dispatched him to the Baltimore Colts for a token payment of $100.

Thanks to the efforts of former star halfback Buddy Young, Lipscomb finally straightened out in Baltimore. After the big tackle played a poor game, Young, who had been treating him with more kindness than Gene had ever known in his life, gave him a heated tounge-lashing. Once he simmered down from that argument, Lipscomb made up his mind to become the best. Gaining pointers from All-Pro teammate Art Donovan, Lipscomb learned how to lower his body to get more leverage into his charge and how to avoid traps. The Baltimore coaching staff also gently prodded him to a better effort. Knowing Big Daddy's reputation as a flashy dresser, they promised him a new hat every time he blocked a kick. In his first year, Lipscomb collected seven hats.

With new friends in a comfortable atmosphere, Eugene Lipscomb blossomed into "Big Daddy" Lipscomb, the most famous defensive lineman in the game. He led the team in tackles in 1957 and was voted All-Pro during the Colt's championship seasons of 1958 and 1959. One of Lipscomb's favorite tricks was to play possum. Just when it looked as if he were blocked out of the hole, he would toss the blocker aside and grab the runner. Besides stuffing the run, Lipscomb could run so fast he once hauled down Detroit's Howard "Hopalong" Cassady from behind after a 50 yard chase. And he loved to nail the quarterback for a loss.

His hilarious stories of the rough-and-tumble days of pro football have made Lipscomb's tutor, Art Donovan, more famous today than when he was a player.

Lipscomb was also far ahead of his time in showmanship. No longer the mean-tempered monster of the Rams, he enjoyed playing the role of the fun-loving, overpowering Big Daddy. Constantly chattering on the field and telling the "little man" across from him what Big Daddy was going to do on the play, he loved to be noticed. As if his size wasn't enough, number 76 could be instantly recognized by the shirt tails that never stayed tucked in and by his high-topped black shoes. Nothing was more fun to him than chasing down and corraling an opposing quarterback or a runner out in the open and then picking him up with a gentle bear hug, a chuckle, and a pat on the rump. "Where you goin', little man?" greeted nearly every running back who ventured into his area. All of his earlier viciousness seemed to have left Lipscomb; in fact, he quit a brief fling at professional wrestling rather than ruin his new clean image.

Still always afraid of failure, Lipscomb worked hard on the field, refusing to coast on his past success. He also tried hard to overcome his neglected upbringing by taking lessons on social skills. Perhaps he learned too well how to socialize because it seemed he was always up for a party. It was a party, in fact, that led to his downfall. Feeling

Big Daddy (76) teamed up with veteran quarterback Bobby Layne (22) to give the Pittsburgh Steelers a rare winning season in 1962.

After playing for one year with an injury, Big Daddy recovered to play what many considered his finest season as he helped the Steelers contend for the championship. Although he still had occasional lapses in play, a number of players considered him to be their toughest opponent. Voted to the Pro Bowl again that season, Lipscomb played perhaps the best game of his career in the All-Star game, blowing past the top offensive linemen in the Western Conference. No one suspected it would be his last game.

No one knows, either, exactly what happened to Big Daddy Lipscomb that spring night. Despite his best efforts, Lipscomb's private life had never completely stabilized, and, after three failed marriages, he kept to himself quite a bit. Despite the glamour of pro football and his reputation as a big spender, he never had that much money—at his peak he was earning about $14,000 a year.

The police said Lipscomb died in a grimy little inner city apartment from a heroin overdose, but his friends refused to believe it. He didn't take drugs, they said, and he was terrified of needles. According to them, just being Big Daddy was enough of a high for him. In the end, however, not even Big Daddy Lipscomb could live up to the legend he had created.

snubbed because some teammates had planned a party and hadn't invited him, Big Daddy reportedly crashed the event and got into a fight with the host.

It was with regret that the Colts decided—for the good of the team, they said—to trade their star tackle. Just before the 1961 season, Lipscomb went to the Pittsburgh Steelers, a dreadful team that was considered the dumping ground for unwanted ballplayers.

GENE LIPSCOMB: BIG DADDY

Born: 1931 in Detroit, Michigan

Size: 6 feet, 6 inches; 285-295 pounds

College: none

Pro Draft: free agent

All-Pro: 1958, 1959, 1961

Pro Bowl: 1959, 1960, 1963

Team Records:

YEAR	TEAM	WINS	LOSSES	TIES	POINTS	POINTS ALLOWED
1953	Los Angeles Rams	8	3	1	366	236
1954	Los Angeles Rams	6	5	1	314	284
1955	Los Angeles Rams	8	3	1	260	231
1956	Baltimore	5	7	0	270	322
1957	Baltimore	7	5	0	303	235
1958	Baltimore	9	3	0	381	203
1959	Baltimore	9	3	0	374	251
1960	Baltimore	6	6	0	288	234
1961	Pittsburgh	6	8	0	240	275
1962	Pittsburgh	9	5	0	312	363

First-Place Finishes: 1955, 1958, 1959

NFL Titles: 1958, 1959

Rosey Grier (76), pass-rushing for the New York Giants, lives life to the fullest, much to the dismay of Washington Redskin quarterback Norm Snead (16).

★★★ 3 ★★★
Roosevelt Grier

The Gentle Giant

If only a little bit of Rosey Grier could have been spread around to the Big Daddy Lipscombs of the world. For as large as Rosey is, the biggest part of him is his joyful energy and enthusiasm. This 6-foot, 5-inch, 290-pound defensive tackle played one of the most violent games for over a decade, yet he emerged with his gentle, sensitive nature still intact. Football was fun to Roosevelt, and so was music, crafts, or just about anything else one could name. Perhaps that was why he is not only as big as two ordinary men but has also crammed more into his life than two ordinary men.

Born in Cuthbert, Georgia, in 1932, Roosevelt, the 7th of 11 children, helped his family scratch out a living as poor farmers. Like Big Daddy Lipscomb, Rosey got up well before dawn to put in a hard work day before school. When they went to town to sell produce such

as watermelons, Rosey wasn't much use, however. He hated to stand out in a crowd so much that he wouldn't shout out to people what he was selling.

Grier had to learn to take charge, though, when his father moved north in 1942. With his older siblings grown and gone, Rosey was in charge of the younger children. After three years of handling such heavy responsibility, he rejoined his father in Roselle, New Jersey.

As an all-around athletic star, Roosevelt earned a football scholarship to Penn State University. While he played the game well enough to attract the attention of the New York Giants, Grier refused to restrict his life to football. Although embarrassed by his poor command of language, he forced himself to speak out in class until he became comfortable. Music was his first love, but after he found his limited formal music background too much of a handicap, he switched his major to education and psychology. Never one to sit still, Rosey also went out for track and set a conference record with a 58-foot shot put.

The Giants drafted Grier in 1955, but they weren't immediately impressed by their new recruit. Roosevelt seemed so kind and polite that it was hard to imagine him shoving anyone. The guy acted as though he was in camp to have fun and obviously didn't believe in knocking himself out in practice. While other players psyched themselves up to a fever pitch before a game, Grier fought back the dry heaves.

When the game started, however, the gigantic rookie would turn aggressive, although never mean. His sheer size provided an anchor to keep such talented but small Giant defensive linemates as 220-pound end Andy Robustelli from being outmuscled, and his aggressive surges often messed up offensive plays before they started. Totally fearless, Grier reminded fans of an overgrown kid playing king-of-the-hill as he hurled himself into the fray.

Although Rosey had such a positive character it was hard to think negative thoughts about him, the Giants had two complaints. One was that Grier's weight kept creeping up past the 300-pound mark, and the Giants thought he would play more effectively at 280 pounds. Incentives and criticism seemed to have no effect until the coaches discovered his weakness. When they hinted that Rosey was letting the team down by being overweight, the selfless tackle dieted in a fit of conscience.

According to many teammates, the other problem was that Grier was just too nice to opponents. Lacking a killer instinct, he couldn't work himself into a rage and would frequently ease up against weaker opponents. Although Rosey raised his level of play a notch against the more capable opponents, on only two occasions did he tap the upper limits of his ability. One opponent made the mistake of publicly announcing that Grier was "easy," and another repeatedly aimed his blocks at Rosey's injured arm. The lesson Grier taught those two on the line of scrimmage was not lost on the rest of the league: Don't get the big guy mad!

In only his second season, 1956, Grier earned All-Pro honors and helped the Giants to their first NFL title in 18 years. But then Uncle Sam came calling, and Roosevelt spent the next season in the U.S. Army. His return in 1958 eased the burden on the defense, and the Giants regained their position at the top of the Eastern Conference. An injury sidelined Grier for most of the historic championship game against the Colts that year, and New York fans couldn't help but wonder if a healthy Grier would have been enough to tip the scales in their favor in the thrilling overtime struggle. New York continued to field one of the NFL's top defenses through the 1962 season, and then Roosevelt was traded to Los Angeles.

For a man who soaked up the joy of working with teammates and who talked about love and togetherness on the field, it was a harsh blow to be suddenly shipped out in exchange for a fairly average offensive tackle. But nothing kept him down for long, and within months Grier's career had reached new heights. With the big man's arrival, the legend of the Fearsome Foursome was born. Flanked by other large, ferocious linemates—Deacon Jones, Merlin Olsen, and Lamar Lundy—Grier found real togetherness in being part of the most feared defensive line in the game.

Although best known for engulfing quarterbacks while they were attempting to pass, the Fearsome Foursome actually specialized in stripping opponents of their running game. During the Foursome's best seasons, 1964 and 1965, they led the NFL in stopping the run and, despite playing in an era of strong running attacks, surrendered just over 100 yards per game.

With Merlin Olsen (above) manning the left defensive tackle position and Grier on the right, the Rams had the rare distinction of starting two future television stars side by side.

Sporting his trademark goatee, Roosevelt Grier catches his breath on the sidelines.

Roosevelt also took advantage of the move to Los Angeles to launch another career: show business. When he wasn't thrashing pro guards on the gridiron, he was strumming a guitar and singing in the recording studio.

During an exhibition game prior to the 1967 season, a ruptured Achilles' tendon shattered Grier's football career, but he wasted no time in moping about it. When a comeback attempt in 1968 failed, Rosey became even more involved in recording and acting. There was something about that round, innocent, bespectacled face on that huge body that, along with his incurable cheerfulness, made him irresistible. He won a regular role on the television series *Daniel Boone* and had his own TV show on a Los Angeles station.

The energetic Grier also found time to become involved in community action and in politics. While campaigning with Robert F. Kennedy in the 1968 presidential primaries, it was Rosey who wrestled Kennedy's assassin, Sirhan Sirhan, to the ground and warded off the blows of an angry mob so the attacker could be brought to justice.

Perhaps the impact that Grier had on football and in his later life can be explained in the image of one of his favorite hobbies: needlepoint. It may have seemed strange to many to see this hulk of a man get so wrapped up in such a craft that he even authored a book on the subject. But Roosevelt never worried about living up to someone else's idea of what a man should be, and he never allowed himself to get stereotyped by his size. So whether he was charging through offensive lines or designing delicate craft patterns, Roosevelt Grier always painted a king-size picture of life at its fullest.

ROOSEVELT GRIER: THE GENTLE GIANT

Born: 1932 in Cuthbert, Georgia

Size: 6 feet, 5 inches; 285-300 pounds

College: Penn State University

Pro Draft: 1955; third round by New York Giants

All-Pro: 1956

Pro Bowl: 1957, 1961

Team Records:

YEAR	TEAM	WINS	LOSSES	TIES	POINTS	POINTS ALLOWED
1955	New York Giants	6	5	1	267	223
1956	New York Giants	8	3	1	264	197
1957	*in military service*					
1958	New York Giants	9	3	0	246	183
1959	New York Giants	10	2	0	284	170
1960	New York Giants	6	4	2	271	261
1961	New York Giants	10	3	1	368	220
1962	New York Giants	11	3	0	448	280
1963	Los Angeles Rams	5	9	0	210	350
1964	Los Angeles Rams	5	7	2	283	339
1965	Los Angeles Rams	4	10	0	269	328
1966	Los Angeles Rams	8	6	0	289	212

First-Place Finishes: 1956, 1958, 1959, 1961, 1962

NFL Titles: 1956

Sherman Plunkett's size became a quarterback's dream and a coach's nightmare.

★★★ 4 ★★★

Sherman Plunkett

Namath's Wall of Protection

Dieters throughout the world can sympathize with Sherman Plunkett. During his career as an offensive tackle in the pros, Plunkett's toughest opponents were not defensive ends but calories. The poor man was one of those people who could gain three pounds by just walking past a bakery. Any hard-earned victory in Plunkett's "Battle of the Bulge" was only temporary, and only through the most agonizing tests of willpower did he manage to hold off defeat for nine seasons.

While critics remember Plunkett only as an immobile mountain, he was actually quite an athlete during his younger days and always showed amazing quickness for a man of his size. In high school in Douglas, Oklahoma, the 280-pound athlete showed the strength and endurance to play tackle on both offense and defense.

Sherman's first weight challenge came at the University of Maryland, and he passed it with flying colors. The 6-foot, 5-inch tackle dieted down to a trim 240 pounds in college and played well enough to receive a tryout with the Cleveland Browns in 1956. But even for a well-conditioned Sherman Plunkett, a pro football career didn't seem possible when he was cut by the team and went on to join the U.S. Army.

During his two years at Fort Dix, New Jersey, Plunkett ran into big Roosevelt Grier and a few other pros who were spending time in the service. After gaining tips from these men, Plunkett felt ready to try the pros again when he left the army in 1958. This time, he caught on with the Baltimore Colts, who were already riding to success on the shoulders of such massive men as Big Daddy Lipscomb, Art Donovan, and Jim

Parker. Plunkett reported at a comfortable 270 pounds, which combined with his time of 5.0 seconds in the 40-yard dash, impressed the Colts as potential All-Pro material.

In Baltimore's two championship seasons of 1958 and 1959, the big tackle played a minor role as a pass protector for the Colts' sensational new quarterback, Johnny Unitas. But as the Colts began to project Plunkett as a major contributor for the near future, they began to grow suspicious of the extra girth around his midsection. After stumbling to a 6-6 mark in 1960, Baltimore did some soul-searching and concluded that, among other things, there was too much of Sherman Plunkett. Prior to training camp in 1961, the Colts offered Sherman a $500 bonus if he would report in at 275 pounds. Losing weight wasn't as easy for Plunkett as it had been, however, and he arrived at camp 25 pounds over the mark. Those extra pounds earned him a ticket out of the NFL, and he spent the next two seasons with the San Diego Chargers in the American Football League (AFL).

Now Coach Weeb Ewbank, who had just joined the New York Jets after being let go by the Colts, remembered his former tackle and decided he was worth another attempt. So Plunkett joined the Jets in 1963. Believing he couldn't be

Until John Hannah's arrival in the 1970s, Jim Parker was widely considered to be football's most dominating blocker.

trusted to do the job by himself, Ewbank offered Sherman's wife, Betty, $1,000 to keep her husband's weight down. Betty tried. Her plan was to give her constantly dieting husband a break at the end of the season and allow him to eat whatever he wanted for two months. After that, it was back to the strict diet. Although the plan wasn't a complete success, Plunkett was able to perform well as the Jets' starting right offensive tackle.

As teams began to loosen up their offenses with more passes, Plunkett became more valuable. While he never lifted weights and wasn't adept at blasting ahead on running plays, he had the size and quick feet to keep himself in front of pass rushers. It was hopeless for a defensive end to try and rush to Plunkett's inside because the big tackle would just shove him into the pile of players. The outside rush was nearly as useless because, as Kansas City Coach Hank Stram commented, "Getting around him is like taking a trip around the world." Despite his easy-going appearance, Plunkett also surprised more than one opponent with a well-placed elbow or forearm when the referee wasn't looking.

After signing Alabama All-American Joe Namath to direct the offense in 1965, the Jets concentrated even more on their passing game. They were willing to overlook some of Plunkett's faults in run-blocking as long as he could keep their expensive new star safe.

When Plunkett reported to camp in 1965, however, it was impossible to overlook his main fault. The scale read 336 pounds, and, bogged down by the weight, Sherman Plunkett lagged far behind his other teammates in running laps. Coach Ewbank had been pushed as far as he could go and stripped Plunkett of his starting job in favor of rookie Sam Walton. He also made the veteran pay his own expenses at camp until he got down to 300 pounds. Plunkett seemed truly baffled by his weight gain, claiming he hardly ever ate anything, and resigned himself to a miserable existence of one meal a day.

Much to Joe Namath's relief, the big tackle won his job back and again provided a solid wall of pass protection. Despite passing more than most teams, in 1965 the Jets offensive line allowed the fewest sacks in the AFL: 17. A year later, Namath enjoyed even more peace and quiet as the Jets gave up only nine sacks all season. And even though his weight had started to creep off the scale again, Plunkett earned All-Pro honors.

Sherman Plunkett hung on for one more season, earning a spot in the AFL All-Star game in 1967, but the end came

As long as Jim Plunkett kept defensive ends away from his fragile knees, Jet quarterback Joe Namath was willing to overlook his tackle's run-blocking problems.

suddenly. AFL teams were discovering the key to beating these monstrous mountains was to turn the pass rush into a foot race. As more and more defensive ends began to beat Plunkett to the outside, he realized the battle was over.

Had he played just one more season, Plunkett might have gained more national exposure. Following the 1968 season, the Jets beat the Colts in Super Bowl II, and the sight of the "Sherman Tank" fending off huge Bubba Smith might have overshadowed even the colorful Namath. Instead, the memory of the largest man ever to star on an NFL offensive team has faded away into obscurity.

SHERMAN PLUNKETT:
NAMATH'S WALL OF PROTECTION

Born: 1933

Size: 6 feet, 5 inches; 270-340 pounds

College: University of Maryland, Eastern Shore

Pro Draft: 1956; sixth round by Cleveland Browns

All-Pro: 1966

Pro Bowl: 1965, 1966, 1967

Team Records:	YEAR	TEAM	WINS	LOSSES	TIES	POINTS	POINTS ALLOWED
	1958	Baltimore	9	3	0	381	203
	1959	Baltimore	9	3	0	374	351
	1960	Baltimore	6	6	0	288	234
	1961	San Diego	7	7	0	301	390
	1962	San Diego	5	9	0	274	423
	1963	New York Jets	5	8	1	249	399
	1964	New York Jets	5	8	1	278	315
	1965	New York Jets	5	8	1	285	303
	1966	New York Jets	6	6	2	322	312
	1967	New York Jets	8	5	1	371	329

First-Place Finishes: 1958, 1959

NFL Titles: 1958, 1959

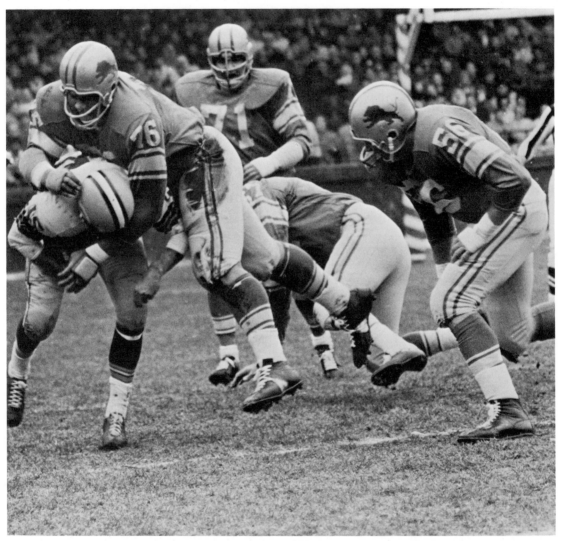

In a famous Thanksgiving Day game, Packer quarterback Bart Starr seemed to be carrying an extra 300 pounds on his back all afternoon.

★★★5★★★

Roger Brown

The Thanksgiving Day Terror

Forget about the Steel Curtain, Dallas' Doomsday defense, or even the Bears' "46" defense of 1985. For 30 minutes on a Thanksgiving Day afternoon in 1962, the Detroit Lions played defense like it had never been played before or since. For those 30 minutes, Roger Brown raged through the finest offensive line in football like windblown fire through a parched forest. On that day, Brown's charge was so ferocious that, had he been able to keep it up throughout his career, the NFL would have folded for lack of able-bodied quarterbacks.

After their success with Les Bingaman, one might have expected the Lions to go all out to find another behemoth to anchor their defensive line. When Roger Brown of the University of Maryland became available in 1960, however, the Lions hemmed and hawed a bit before finally drafting him in the fourth round.

Coaches could never tell about those gentle 300-pound speech majors who had failed to dominate their opponents in the college ranks. Did they have either the toughness or the athletic ability to succeed in the pros?

It didn't take long, however, for the Lions to discover that the Surry County, Virginia, native had more to offer than just shoulders too wide to squeeze through an ordinary doorway. Defying the laws of gravity, Roger Brown could run fast enough to catch running backs from behind. As for his toughness, the mild-mannered, bespectacled book-worm seemed to change into an entirely different creature by game day. Beginning to psych himself up the day before a game, Brown would stew about all of the players he had seen injured on the field and would convince himself that his opponent was trying to do the same to him. The result was that Brown, in his own words, became "a person I wouldn't like to meet on the field." One of his tactics earned him the nickname "Bell Ringer." Back in the days when this was legal, Brown would start his charge with a whack to the opponent's

helmet, which one man described as similar to being kicked in the head by a mule. Then, when the game was over, Brown would settle back into his old docile self. He once said the part of football he enjoyed the most was lying for hours in a hot tub after the game.

While Bingaman had aimed to keep himself as big as possible, Brown constantly searched for the right blend of weight and speed, which he seemed to achieve at a few ounces under 300 pounds. When asked about his strengths as a defender, Brown would speak about neither size nor speed but instead prefered to discuss the finer points of his craft. Brown prided himself on knowing the techniques of holding his ground and getting past a blocker, and he spent a great deal of time learning to read the little offensive clues that tell where the play was going. Yet, on occasion, he could abandon all the subtle parts of the game and simply crash through the blocking. Once, following a trade, he was rushed into service without knowing any of his new team's defensive signals, and he still performed admirably.

As a rookie in 1960, Brown was installed next to All-Pro Alex Karras to give the Lions the best—and most nearsighted—tackle combination in the NFL. Unlike most mega-linemen, Brown's strength was not in plugging up the

A close-up view of what Starr saw, minus helmet.

Yet another tackle-turned-actor, Alex Karras provided a more consistent level of excellence than teammate Roger Brown did.

middle but in his furious pass rush. Never was that more evident than in 1962. Vince Lombardi's mighty Green Bay Packers had reached their peak that season and boasted no fewer than 11 All-Pros. Nearly lost amid the glowing praises of the Packers, however, was the fact that, led by their plundering defense, the Detroit Lions played just as well.

Early in the season, the Lions had the Packers beaten on their own turf, only to see their quarterback throw a foolish interception at the end of the game to hand the victory to Green Bay. That win gave the Packers clear sailing toward a divisional title, and they rolled into Detroit for a Thanksgiving Day rematch with 10-0 mark. There they discovered a Lion defense that had been seething ever since their earlier bitter loss. Although the Packers thought they were ready for the contest, there was no way anyone could have prepared for the 300-pound locomotive that would be bearing down on them.

No quarterback in pro football could have felt safer than Green Bays' Bart Starr. Four of the five linemen protecting him—center Jim Ringo, guards Fuzzy Thurston and Jerry Kramer, and tackle Forest Gregg—were All-Pros. Yet, Roger Brown, ably assisted by Karras and a host of blitzing linebackers, totally wiped out the great Packer line. One bewildered Packer later said the Lions "were past us before we could find them." Fullback Jim Taylor, the NFL's top runner, scratched out only three yards in the first half, and Starr was buried time and again while attempting to pass.

With Detroit holding a 14-0 lead, Roger Brown single-handedly put the game out of reach. First, he engulfed Starr far behind the line of scrimmage, causing the usually cool and collected quarterback to fumble. Then Detroit's

Sam Williams scooped up the loose ball and ran into the end zone for a touchdown. Less than two minutes later, Brown roared through a double-team block by All-Pros Thurston and Taylor to trap the shell-shocked Starr in the end zone for a safety. By the time the half had ended, Starr had lost 93 yards attempting to pass, and the Lions led, 23 to 0! Although the Lions eased up in the second half, they finished with 11 sacks and 110 yards in losses. Five of those sacks belonged to Roger Brown.

The memories of that one terrifying afternoon were probably enough to get Brown selected to the Pro Bowl game for the next six seasons. But it was hardly the only great performance of his career. In 1962, Detroit's defense led the NFL in sack yardage and in stopping the run, and they led the NFL in sacks in 1965 In both seasons, Brown was a key reason.

When the Los Angeles Rams' Fearsome Foursome was dissolved by the career-ending injury to Roosevelt Grier in 1967, the Rams immediately filled those enormous shoes with the equally enormous feet of Roger Brown. During the three seasons in which Brown blended his talents with those of Merlin Olsen, Deacon Jones, and Lamar Lundy, Los Angeles won 32 games and lost only 7. As usual, whenever Brown was around,

quarterbacks could expect no peace, and in 1968 the Rams piled up an impressive total of 51 sacks to lead the NFL. Just as had been the case with Detroit's defense, the Fearsome Foursome was never better than when Roger Brown was in the middle of the action.

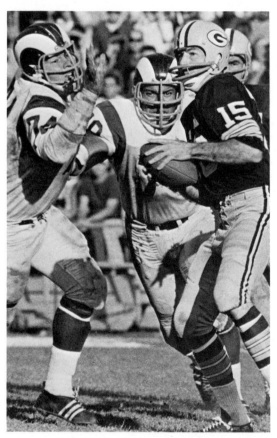

No matter for whom he played, Brown (center) seemed to have it in for Bart Starr. Here, he races Ram teammate Merlin Olsen for the chance to bury the Packer leader.

ROGER BROWN: THE THANKSGIVING DAY TERROR

Born: 1937 in Surrey County, Virginia

Size: 6 feet, 5 inches; 300 pounds

College: University of Maryland, Eastern Shore

Pro Draft: 1960; fourth round by Detroit Lions

All-Pro: 1962, 1963

Pro Bowl: 1963, 1964, 1965, 1966, 1967, 1968

Team Records:

YEAR	TEAM	WINS	LOSSES	TIES	POINTS	POINTS ALLOWED
1960	Detroit	7	7	0	239	212
1961	Detroit	8	5	1	270	258
1962	Detroit	11	3	0	315	177
1963	Detroit	5	8	1	326	265
1964	Detroit	7	5	2	280	260
1965	Detroit	6	7	1	257	295
1966	Detroit	4	9	1	206	259
1967	Los Angeles Rams	11	1	2	398	196
1968	Los Angeles Rams	10	3	1	312	200
1969	Los Angeles Rams	11	3	0	320	243

First-Place Finishes: 1967, 1969

NFL Titles: none

Barely visible behind a white-uniformed tidal wave, New York's Joe Namath is about to be swamped by the largest tackle tandem ever to play in the NFL. Between them, Ernie Ladd (left) and Buck Buchanan (right) hurled 600 fast-moving pounds at the quarterback.

★★★6★★★
Ernie Ladd

Football's Most Dangerous Man

Had Ernie Ladd reported for pro football during the age of computers, it might have taken a decade for scouting systems to recover from the shock. Imagine the smoke, sparks, blown fuses, and short circuits as the poor machine tried to process measurements that were beyond belief. According to the tape measure, it was a 54-inch journey around Ladd's chest, which tapered nicely to an athletic-looking 40-inch waist. Ladd's neck measured 19 inches. His biceps were 20 inches and his calves, 20, and he wore a size 17EEE shoe. Put all of that on a 6-foot, 9-inch frame, and you have 315 pounds of well-conditioned muscle. Then add on the fact that Ladd could outrun most linemen—and had a fierce, mean attitude on the football field—and you have a man who was more than "potentially the greatest lineman to play the game." You have a

man who was very nearly too dangerous to be turned loose in even the rugged ranks of the NFL.

Ernest Ladd was born in Orange, Texas, in 1938. With a father who tipped the scales at 265 pounds and a 6-foot mother, no one was surprised when Ernie outgrew his clothing faster than his friends. Other children used to ridicule Ladd's enormous feet, but the rest of his body caught up so quickly that soon it wasn't wise to laugh at him, especially given his temper.

Following in the footsteps of his idol, a powerful football star named Tank Younger, Ernie attended Grambling State University in Louisiana. With his speed and natural coordination, Ladd had dreams of catching passes and perhaps playing a little basketball during the off-season, as he had done in high school. But he kept growing until the

47

only logical place for a man of his size was in the middle of a football team's defensive line at tackle.

Although Grambling was a small school, alumni such as Green Bay's All-Pro defensive lineman Willie Davis had given it top priority in pro football scouting files. After he was named the team's most valuable lineman in 1960, Ladd, with still a year of college eligibility remaining, was drafted by both the NFL Chicago Bears and the San Diego Chargers of the new American Football League. A secret war for college talent was raging between the two leagues, and Ernie was caught in the middle of it. The Chargers talked him into meeting the team's players, who were on a plane waiting to take off. Then, before Ladd could pull himself away, the plane was in the air. While the Bears tried to locate their prospect, the Chargers entertained him for a week in Los Angeles and persuadad him to accept their modest offer of $10,000.

After a brief time at training camp, some of the best minds in pro football were raving about this new prospect. Charger line coach Chuck Noll, who would later guide Pittsburgh's awesome Steel Curtain defensive line, said that Ladd could be as good as he wanted to be.

The youngster seemed determined not to let anyone stand in his way of suc-

Obviously, Ladd was not the kind of person you wanted to have angry with you!

cess. His own coach admitted that Ladd seemed to have more than just a mean streak: he could be downright sadistic. Opposing linemen who suffered cracked helmets and headaches from his wrath agreed. Big Ernie's main strategy was to go for the man with the ball and break down anyone unfortunate enough to be between him and the ball carrier. If knocked off his feet, he simply rolled over, and clawed, thrashed, and crawled his way to the ball.

During the early 1960s, Ladd teamed with a powerful young defensive end, Earl Faison, to give San Diego a defensive line even larger than the Rams' Fearsome Foursome—and some AFL fans claimed they were just as good. With Faison and Ladd spurring each other

When Earl Faison joined Ladd at San Diego, a match with the Chargers became not only frustrating but hazardous to one's health.

on with a personal rivalry, the Charger line was easily the best in the AFL. During 1961, the sight of enormous Ernie and his friends panicked the enemy quarterbacks into throwing the ball up for grabs. As a result, the Charger defensive backs collected an astounding 49 interceptions. In a wildly offensive league, it was the Charger defense that led the club to four divisional titles in the five-year reign of Ernie Ladd. Ladd and Faison probably reached their peak during the 1963 season when the Chargers destroyed the Boston Patriots in the championship game, 51 to 10. Al Davis, the mastermind of the Raider organization, called Ernie "the most dynamic defensive force in pro football."

Yet, somehow the fear that Ladd injected into opponents seldom translated into All-Pro votes. Only in 1964 and 1965 was he acclaimed an AFL All-Pro, a meager trophy case for a man with such physical gifts. While many giants such as Rosey Grier and Bubba Smith were handicapped by their peaceful natures, Ernie may have had the opposite problem. Not only did he have little consideration for an opponent's feelings, he also battled his own team and even the league. When the AFL told him his beard had to go, Ladd was furious. And when the Chargers refused to pay him what he thought he deserved,

Ladd publicly criticized the San Diego organization. He had trouble dredging up any kind of team spirit, and his concentration drifted away during games. That stormy relationship ended in 1965 when he played out his option and signed with the Houston Oilers.

Just when Ladd should have been starting to reach his peak, however, he began to fade out of the starting lineup and out of the memories of all but a few veteran AFL fans. Ironically, it was his greatest asset—his overpowering size and strength—that did him in. No offensive blocker could hope to budge such a tower of power with their normal blocking techniques. The only way they could slow him down was to "cut" him, a football term for blocking low. Game after game, Ernie took brutal shots to the most vulnerable part of a player's body—his knees. As his knees gave out, Ladd found it harder to move, and his appearances in enemy backfields became rare. After a year with the Oilers, Ernie moved on to the Chiefs, where he joined another Grambling star, 285-pound Buck Buchanan, to form an intimidating wall. But Ladd's bad knees hurt and restricted him so much that, after a few mediocre seasons in Kansas City, he gave up football in 1968 at the age of 29.

Of all the larger-than-life stories about Ladd, perhaps the most astounding are

Buck Buchanan anchored the Kansas City defense that stifled the Minnesota Vikings in Super Bowl IV.

the reports of how much fuel his massive body needed. While at Grambling, Ernie once wolfed down 52 pancakes. A light lunch might start with 10 pork chops, and it took 2 steaks, 8 eggs, 16 strips of bacon, 8 slices of toast, and 6 glasses of orange juice to get him ready for a football game. Even in those pre-inflation days, San Diego had to shell out $50 a day to feed Ernie. For a brief time, that was money well spent as pro football may never again see a man quite as frightening as Ernie Ladd.

ERNIE LADD: FOOTBALL'S MOST DANGEROUS MAN

Born: 1938 in Orange, Texas

Size: 6 feet, 9 inches; 315 pounds

College: Grambling State University

Pro Draft: 1961; fourth round by Chicago Bears & 15th round by San Diego Chargers

All-Pro: 1964, 1965

Pro Bowl: 1963, 1964, 1965, 1966

Team Records:	YEAR	TEAM	WINS	LOSSES	TIES	POINTS	POINTS ALLOWED
	1961	San Diego	12	2	0	396	219
	1962	San Diego	4	10	0	314	392
	1963	San Diego	11	3	0	399	256
	1964	San Diego	8	5	1	341	300
	1965	San Diego	9	2	3	340	227
	1966	Houston	3	11	0	335	396
	1967	Kansas City*	9	5	0	408	254
	1968	Kansas City	12	2	0	371	170

*started season with Houston

First-Place Finishes: 1961, 1963, 1964, 1965

AFL Titles: 1963

Easy-going Bubba Smith lacked the killer instinct to live up to his reputation as an annihilator.

★★★ 7 ★★★
Bubba Smith

Legend Before His Time

Maybe it's something in the water in Orange, Texas. In 1948, 10 years after Ernie Ladd was born there, another Texan of epic proportions made his initial appearance in that town. Although not quite as mammoth as Ladd, Bubba Smith blazed a much wider trail of notoriety. While most linemen developed slowly into stardom, Bubba had grown into a legend by his junior year of college. The pro career that followed fell far short of the expectations for him, but it's doubtful any human could have lived up to the advance billing that hung over Bubba throughout his brief career. After all, when a pro football general manager raves about a player as having "nearly as much potential as the atom bomb," nothing he does will ever be good enough.

Charles Aaron Smith grew up with all the right ingredients to excel in foot-

ball. Not only did "Bubba"—as he was nicknamed at an early age—have size and speed, he also didn't have to leave the dinner table to find expert coaching. Bubba's father coached a high school football team in Beaumont, Texas, with such dedication and skill that it was considered a poor season when they lost a game or two. His mother, who had earned a doctorate in education, knew the game nearly as well. And with some equally large brothers around, Bubba grew up learning how to butt heads with pro-sized people.

It was at Michigan State University that Bubba Smith's reputation grew even larger than his 6-foot, 7-inch, 285-pound body. After watching the big tackle manhandle opponents, a Spartan public relations person encouraged students to take up a new cheer: "Kill, Bubba, kill!" Supported by a splendid collection of talent such as lineman Harold Lucas and rover back George Webster, it did seem as though Bubba could steamroll over anyone. "Kill, Bubba, kill!" chants rang through the stadium whenever the number-one ranked Spartans played at home in 1965 and 1966.

During the 1966 season, in a battle many called "the game of the century," Michigan State took on a Notre Dame team that many boasted was its finest in many years. Smith's reputation as a ruthless destroyer was not harmed when Notre Dame's quarterback and center had to be helped off the field after brutal collisions with the Michigan State monster. At the end of the game, Bubba screamed in disgust at the Irish, who were settling for a tie instead of going for a win.

In short, Smith seemed exactly like the type of wild bull who might scatter pro offenses to the winds. Built up to over 290 pounds by the end of his college career, Bubba impressed Baltimore's respected coach, Don Shula, as a player who "comes along once in a lifetime," and in 1967 the Colts eagerly used their number-one draft choice to claim him. Big Bubba's fearsome feats were so well known that even the grizzled Colt veterans decided to pass up the usual teasing and tormenting of rookies. Bigger and faster than their old teammate, Big Daddy Lipscomb, Smith had the Colts gaping open-mouthed at some of his one-on-one moves.

Once the season had started, however, the cry of "Kill, Bubba, kill!" hushed to a whisper. Bubba wasn't killing anyone. In fact, he seemed to be fighting just to hold his ground, and smaller opponents tried the same low chops to Bubba's legs that had floored Ernie Ladd —and with similar success. Teammates complained the rookie didn't seem that interested in the game and didn't study

Years later, Smith expressed disgust over the blood-thirsty mentality of Michigan State fans.

Even Smith's stance shows concern for his knee, which was in constant danger of injury from chop blocks by smaller players.

In 1968, however, the Colts moved Bubba out of the middle of the field to left end where he wouldn't be attacked from all angles by low-flying guards. At end, he was freed from some running play responsibilities and could concentrate on what he did best—rushing the quarterback. Slimming down to the 275-pound range, Bubba provided the pass rush on a defense that allowed only 144 points during the season. Unfortunately, however, the Colts' year was ruined by a humiliating loss to the New York Jets in the Super Bowl.

After working with his family through the hot Texas summer, Bubba reported for the 1970 season in the best shape of his life. The result was a Super Bowl championship won by the Colts' defense in a bruising battle with the Dallas Cowboys. With nine sacks and four blocked field goals the following season, Smith seemed to be making strides toward living up to his impossible reputation. Not only did he apply pressure from his position, but his size hid linebackers, who could dart from behind him on a surprise blitz.

During a 1972 exhibition game, Bubba was chasing a runner toward the sidelines when he got tangled up in an out-of-bounds marker. When he fell, his knee was so badly injured that he missed the entire season. Fighting hard to come

game films. The Colts had expected a fire-breathing dragon, but Smith had turned out to gentle, almost timid.

For the first time in his life, the bewildered Bubba was banished to the bench while a meaner Smith—veteran Billy Ray—took over his starting tackle spot. Depressed and confused, the rookie nearly quit in midseason. Indeed, some of his teammates wondered if he had. On special teams, Bubba was always the last man out on the field—if he remembered to go out at all. Once he even forgot to remove his eyeglasses before entering a game.

back from the devastating injury, in 1973 Smith was traded to the Oakland Raiders. But the damage to his knee had been too great. Bubba lasted two unspectacular years before giving it up and following Rosey Grier to an acting career.

Bubba Smith and football fans had been victims of false advertising. Smith had performed well during his seven pro seasons—and certainly had the physical ability to have done better—but the title of "Killer" could hardly have been tagged on a less deserving person. Bubba often said he wished he were mean, but that just wasn't his nature. Because he was forced to try to live up to others' ideas of what he should be, Bubba's heart was not in the game. Rarely playing with emotion, he considered football a job, not a sport. While the fantasy Bubba Smith, the quarterback-stalking monster, might have been more fun for the fans, it was a role that Bubba just couldn't play.

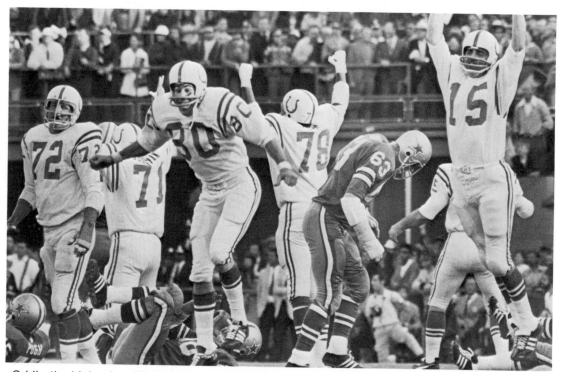

Oddly, the highpoint of Smith's career came on a rare offensive play. Here, Bubba (78) celebrates after blocking for the last-second field goal that won Super Bowl V.

BUBBA SMITH: LEGEND BEFORE HIS TIME

Born: 1948 in Orange, Texas

Size: 6 feet, 7 inches; 270-295 pounds

College: Michigan State University

Pro Draft: 1967; first round by Baltimore Colts

All-Pro: 1971

Pro Bowl: 1971, 1972

Team Records:	YEAR	TEAM	WINS	LOSSES	TIES	POINTS	POINTS ALLOWED
	1967	Baltimore	11	1	2	394	198
	1968	Baltimore	13	1	0	402	144
	1969	Baltimore	8	5	1	279	268
	1970	Baltimore	11	2	1	321	234
	1971	Baltimore	10	4	0	313	140
	1972	*injured*					
	1973	Oakland	9	4	1	292	175
	1974	Oakland	12	2	0	355	228
	1975	Houston	10	4	0	293	226
	1976	Houston	5	9	0	222	273

First-Place Finishes: 1968, 1970, 1973, 1974

NFL Titles: 1968

AFC Titles: 1970

Super Bowl Titles: 1970

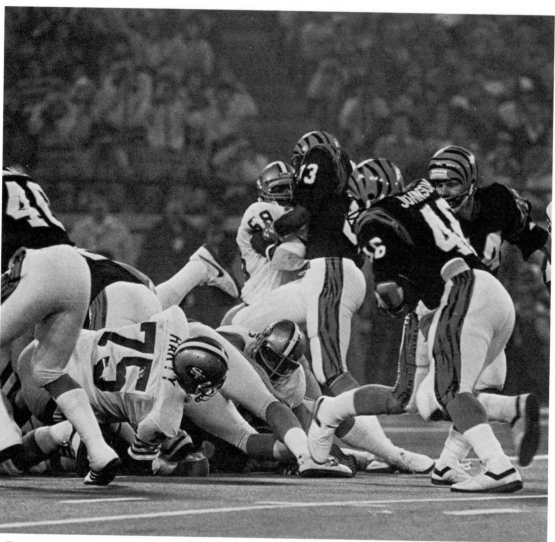

Football in its rawest form: thundering Pete Johnson charges toward the heart of the San Francisco 49ers massed goal-line defense in Super Bowl XVI.

★★★ 8 ★★★
Pete Johnson

The Backfield Bull

In the late 1800s when college football coaches took advantage of some basic physics to design mass momentum plays, the most notorious play was the flying wedge. In the flying wedge, all 10 blockers joined hands in a "V" formation with the ball carrier tucked in the middle and took a running start at the defense. The simple principle was that a large amount of mass concentrated in a small area and moving at a high speed would be very difficult to stop. This battering-ram approach was so powerful it led to many injuries—and even deaths—so it was banned in 1894.

In following the history of pro football, it almost appears as though football officials outlawed not only the flying wedge but the entire principle of mass momentum. The largest men are placed in a stationary position on the line of scrimmage where they can wrestle and shove and tie each other up while the little guys prance around with the ball. On short yardage occasions, most teams pay token respect to the mass momentum concept by putting in a "large" running back to carry the ball. Even the largest of these running backs, however, generally weigh 40 to 50 pounds less than the linemen they run against. For example, Miami's Larry Csonka and Washington's John Riggins, the classic bulls of the backfield, didn't tip the scales past 235. And so it was Pete Johnson who had to prove that physics hadn't changed and that it was still true that 280 pounds of mass moving at a sprinter's speed packed a mighty wallop.

Willie James Hammock was born in Fort Valley, Georgia, in 1954—a fact that wouldn't be of interest except that Pete Johnson and Willie James Hammock are the same person. Willie grew up on a farm with his great-grandparents and was tagged with the nickname "Pete" at a young age. His other last name, Johnson, came about because of his exceptional talent in football. Even at the age of 12, Pete Johnson could play well enough to help the high school team. But because the high school didn't want it known they were using such a young kid, Willie Hammock played under the name of Pete Johnson. Pete may well have been the only athlete in the United States to have played six years of high school football! College scouts were certainly confused. When they tried to recruit Johnson during his "senior" year, they found out he was only a sophomore.

After moving to Long Island, New York, for his final year of high school, Pete accepted a football scholarship at Ohio State University. There, his dual identity really fouled up the records, as he attended class under the name Willie Hammock and played football as Pete Johnson. When there was no person named Pete Johnson enrolled in classes, the football team had a tough time proving that he was eligible to play. Because of this, he finally settled on Pete Johnson as his chosen name.

The Buckeyes seemed to have struck a bargain between Johnson and his backfield mate, Archie Griffin. Griffin

The Buckeye merit badges plastered across Johnson's helmet show he was not idle while playing at Ohio State.

Pete (left) and his Ohio State backfield mate, Archie Griffin (right), took their act from Columbus to Cincinnati. With the Bengals, however, it was Johsnon who won top billing.

could have the yards and the headlines as long as Johnson got the touchdowns. While Griffin shattered yardage marks and captured two Heisman Trophy awards, Johnson set a Big Ten Conference career record by scoring 58 touchdowns.

At 6 feet and 259 pounds, Pete Johnson did not fit the pro description of a running back. His square build made him look slow and clumsy, but the Cincinnati Bengals were intrigued by the fact that, even with the extra weight,

Johnson could run the 100-yard dash in 9.9 seconds. They made him their second round draft choice in 1977 and reunited him with his old friend Archie Griffin in the backfield.

After leading the club in rushing during his rookie year and continuing to do so for the next several years, Johnson could have expected acclaim as a top NFL runner. But it was as though no one took such a large person seriously as a running back. Along with

Pete's own hatred of publicity, Johnson was one of the largest and best kept secrets in the game.

Opponents who had made the mistake of getting in his way, however, were well aware of who Pete was. Running low to the ground with both hands wrapped around the ball, Johnson was like a giant bowling ball. He rarely fumbled and never got knocked backwards, and not even the largest tacklers could wrap their arms around his 29-inch thighs. Pittsburgh's All-Pro linebacker Jack Lambert, who made himself well-acquainted with NFL runners, declared Johnson the toughest back he ever had to bring down. Lambert had probably reached that opinion in one game incident at the Steelers three-yard line. The Steeler defense had plugged all the holes, but Johnson blasted right into the pile and churned the whole mass of bodies into the end zone for a touchdown.

Despite the success he enjoyed playing 30 to 40 pounds heavier than the biggest NFL back, Johnson seemed locked in an endless battle with the scale. When he arrived at the Bengal training camp in 1980 weighing 270 pounds, Coach Forrest Gregg just gaped at him. Johnson made some half-hearted efforts to reach the weight goal his coach had set for him—245 pounds—

but played above 260 most of the time. An independent spirit who seemed able to ignore all outside pressure, Johnson explained his position on weight by saying, "When a truck hits you, who gets hurt?" One of Pete's goals as a runner was to give anyone who tried to tackle him the worst of the collision.

When the Bengals defied the experts by marching to the 1981 Super Bowl, it was Johnson who provided much of the offense. That season, he used his breakaway speed to gain 1,077 yards and his power to score 16 touchdowns, both Bengal records. Then just to show he was more than a pile driver, he also collected 46 pass receptions. By the end of the next season, the 28-year-old fullback owned Cincinnati career records in rushing yards, touchdowns, and total offense. Johnson didn't seem particularly impressed by his statistics, however. "I don't be counting, he said. "I just be playing."

After slipping into the trap of drug experimentation, Johnson's value dropped dramatically. In 1984, he was peddled to the San Diego Chargers, who passed him along to the Miami Dolphins after three games. Although quarterback Dan Marino and tiny wide receivers Mark Duper and Mark Clayton received most of the publicity, big Pete

Johnson, coach Forrest Gregg, quarterback Ken Anderson (14), and tight end Dan Ross shrug off the tension as they prepare to play San Francisco in Super Bowl XVI.

Johnson played a major role in powering the Dolphins to Super Bowl XIX. Despite gaining only 205 yards that year while playing the role of designated scorer, Johnson crashed into the end zone 12 times in short yardage situations.

By this time, one would have thought Johnson would have persuaded all the experts that someone could be huge and still be a running back. But in 1985, his pro career came to an end instead when he didn't lose the weight the Dolphins had expected him to lose. Pete Johnson had discovered that when you're battling nearly a century-old tradition of small running backs, performance wasn't always enough.

Pete Johnson

PETE JOHNSON: THE BACKFIELD BULL

Born: 1954 in Fort Valley, Georgia

Size: 6 feet; 255-280 pounds

College: Ohio State University

Pro Draft: 1977; second round by Cincinnati Bengals

All-Pro: none

Pro Bowl: 1982

Individual Records: YEAR	TEAM	RUSHING			PASS RECEIVING			TDs
		Attempts	Yds.	Ave.	Catches	Yds.	Ave.	
1977	Cincinnati	153	585	3.8	5	49	9.8	4
1978	Cincinnati	180	762	4.2	31	236	7.6	7
1979	Cincinnati	243	865	3.6	24	154	6.4	15
1980	Cincinnati	186	747	4.0	21	172	8.2	7
1981	Cincinnati	274	1,077	3.9	46	320	7.0	16
1982	Cincinnati	156	622	4.0	31	267	8.6	7
1983	Cincinnati	210	763	3.6	15	129	8.6	14
1984	Miami*	87	205	2.4	0	0	0	12

*started season with San Diego

First-Place Finishes: 1981, 1984

AFC Titles: 1981, 1984

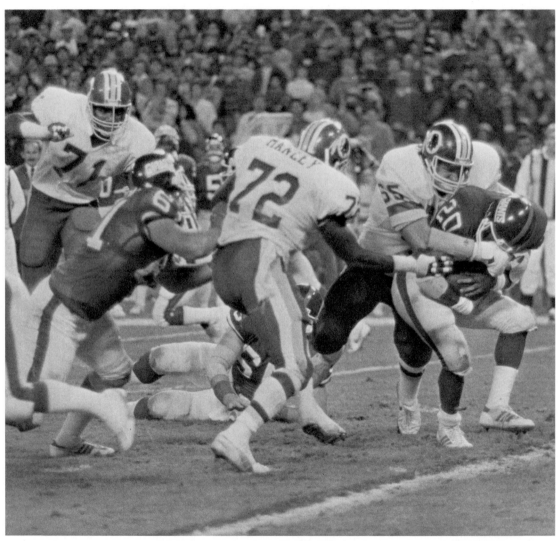

There is no hope for New York Giant star Joe Morris this time as he is engulfed by the
Redskins' bastion against the run, Dave Butz.

★★★9★★★

Dave Butz

The Invisible Giant

Thanks to the Washington Redskins, it can now be considered a compliment rather than an insult for a large person to be called a "hog." While other NFL teams kept a wary eye on their players' weights in 1982, the Redskins unashamedly bellied up to the line of scrimmage and leaned and shoved and pounded their way past trimmer foes to win a Super Bowl title. While the enormous offensive linemen proudly nicknamed themselves "the Hogs," the biggest and the most experienced—and possibly the best Hog of all—played quietly in the defensive line. Given the public's fascination with giants of the gridiron, it's baffling that someone as large and as talented as Dave Butz could play almost unnoticed for a decade.

When he measured 24 inches at birth in Lafayette, Alabama, in 1950, Dave served notice that he was going to cost his family a few more groceries than the average kid. At the age of three, the fast-growing youngster was big enough to handle the steering of a two-ton truck while his father pitched hay out the back. By the time Butz was in the fourth grade, he had swelled to 150 pounds, with no signs of slowing down.

During high school in Park Ridge, Illinois, Butz used his size and remarkable coordination to win high school All-American honors two years in a row in football as well as the state shot put title. He also showed how dangerous it was to get in his way on the basketball court when he destroyed a glass backboard during a slam dunk.

After high school, Dave started for the Purdue University Boilermakers for three seasons and won a scattering of All-American honors. But the 6-foot, 7-inch, 295-pound defensive tackle really made the scouts sit up and take notice when he earned Most Valuable Player honors in two post-season college All-Star games. His dominance persuaded the St. Louis Cardinals to draft him with their first-round choice in 1973.

Even though Butz was named to the NFL All-Rookie team in 1973, the Cardinals felt they weren't getting their money's worth out of him. After a knee injury limited him to just one game in 1974, St. Louis allowed Butz to play out his option. The Washington Redskins jumped at the chance to sign him, but they blanched when the NFL presented the check. In exchange for the mammoth tackle, they were forced to give up two first-round draft choices and a second-round choice. That compensation deal was the largest ever awarded by the NFL. While some of the Redskins grumbled about the high-priced, unproven newcomer, none of them griped more than the equipment manager, who was given the harrowing task of trying to find equipment to fit the 303-pound man. If coming up with a size 52 extra-large jersey with a 19-inch neck wasn't hard enough, the Redskins also had to find someone to make a special order size 12½EEEEEEE shoe!

Once the shock of the settlement wore off, however, Butz managed to settle into the background. Slowly he worked his way into the lineup, sharing a starting position with Bill Brundige for a couple of seasons before taking over in 1978. That year, Dave was voted the Redskins' Defensive Player of the Year.

Even when Dave was playing at his best, however, it took an astute observer to notice him because his greatest strength was standing his ground while taking on two blockers at a time. Although opponents often seemed to run into a pile of bodies near the line of scrimmage, it wasn't always obvious that big Dave had caused the logjam. Butz preferred to concentrate on team defense, staying back and manning his position rather than trying for the flashy big play. As a result, the Pro Bowl went on year after year without one of the game's best defensive players.

It may have been the example of this colossus-in-the-middle who inspired Washington to take a chance on another 300-pounder, Joe Jacoby. Jacoby had accomplished so little during his career at the University of Louisville that no one drafted him in 1981, and a Redskin assistant had to talk head coach Joe Gibbs into keeping him on the roster. But two months into his rookie season when Jacoby cracked the starting lineup, the Hogs were born. With Butz anchoring the defense and Jacoby and fellow Hogs such as Russ Grimm and Mark May

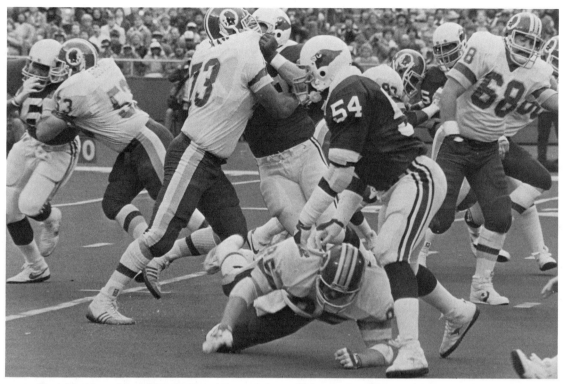

Redskin Hogs Mark May (73) and Russ Grimm (68) pound away at the St. Louis Cardinals.

plowing paths for John Riggins, Washington marched into the Super Bowl at the end of the 1982 season.

In that game, it was Butz who pounced on a key fumble that kept the Miami Dolphins from building a big first-half lead. He also stuffed the Dolphin running attack and helped harrass Miami quarterbacks into a dismal showing of only four completed passes in 17 attempts. Meanwhile, fullback John Riggins rooted out 166 yards in 38 carries—mostly behind the blocks of the massive Jacoby —to grind out the victory.

Butz enjoyed an even finer season in 1983 when the Redskins repeated as NFC champs. Not only did he continue to clog up the middle, helping the Redskins' become the NFL's top ranked team in defending against the run, he also forced five fumbles and led the club with 11½ sacks. That type of performance finally let the NFL's biggest secret out of the bag.

The most durable of pro football's giants continued to anchor the Redskin defense through 1986, gaining awards and honors that had escaped him during his first decade of play. At long last, Dave Butz could step out of his role as the 300-pound invisible man.

Left: Even without shoulder pads, Butz fills out the biggest uniform the Redskins can find. Below: Miami tailback Tony Nathan (22) has about one-half second to escape the tackle before an onrushing Dave Butz (65) flattens him. Butz bottled up the Dolphins' inside running game in this Super Bowl XVII win.

DAVE BUTZ: THE INVISIBLE GIANT

Born: 1950 in Lafayette, Alabama

Size: 6 feet, 7 inches; 305 pounds

College: Purdue University

Pro Draft: 1973; first round by St. Louis Cardinals

All-Pro: 1983

Pro Bowl: 1984

Team Records:	YEAR	TEAM	WINS	LOSSES	TIES	POINTS	POINTS ALLOWED
	1973	St. Louis	4	9	1	286	385
	1974	St. Louis	10	4	0	285	218
	1975	Washington	8	6	0	325	276
	1976	Washington	10	4	0	291	217
	1977	Washington	9	5	0	196	189
	1978	Washington	8	8	0	273	283
	1979	Washington	10	6	0	348	295
	1980	Washington	6	10	0	261	293
	1981	Washington	8	8	0	347	349
	1982	Washington	8	1	0	190	128
	1983	Washington	14	2	0	541	332
	1984	Washington	11	5	0	426	310
	1985	Washington	10	6	0	297	312
	1986	Washington	12	4	0	368	296

First-Place Finishes: 1974, 1982, 1983, 1984

NFC Titles: 1982

Super Bowl Titles: 1982

The original "whaleback" celebrates his first NFL touchdown while the stunned Green Bay Packers try to recover from the shock of defending against a 320-pound ball carrier.

★★★ 10 ★★★

William Perry

The Refrigerator

Among the reams of statistics cranked out by the National Football League, one can find a dull, brief entry summing up a rookie running back's debut. The record shows that on October 21, 1985, a Chicago Bear reserve named William Perry gained four yards in two carries against the San Francisco 49ers. While hardly exciting stuff, that performance launched William Perry into the limelight as one of football's most popular players.

Perry was no ordinary running back. He was The Refrigerator, and, once he clamped his hands on the ball, the nicely ordered, computer-scouted, poker-faced world of the NFL was tossed into the garbage compactor. For those who thought the pro game had gotten too stuffy, too mechanical, and too boring, The Refrigerator provided a splash of color. Make that a tidal wave of color.

When asked to describe his primary weakness, what other pro player would answer, "Cheeseburgers"?

Since his arrival in Aiken, South Carolina, in 1962, the 10th of 12 children, William Perry has taken up more than his share of space on this planet. With a birth weight of 13½ pounds, William managed to stand out even among a family of large people—all 250 to 300 pounds. There weren't many luxuries in the Perry family, but there was always food. Little William ate so much and grew so huge that, despite his friendly nature, his mother was always afraid he would hurt somebody.

What made Perry *really* unusual was that his enormous body didn't seem aware of the laws of gravity. Carrying 315 pounds on a relatively short 6-foot, 2-inch frame, he could jump high enough to dunk a basketball! At Aiken High

Neither the Kentucky Wildcats nor a Clemson uniform could contain The Refrigerator. Pity the ball carrier!

School, he averaged 18 points a game on the hardcourt and ran the 100-yard dash in 11.4 seconds. And even though he played one of the least glamorous positions on the field—nose tackle—his blend of size, speed, and coordination made him an instant legend. Just for the fun of it, Perry was allowed to carry the ball a few times for Aiken. Little did he know the bedlam he would cause when he took to the backfield again five years later.

At Clemson University, Perry continued to grow into the most awesome defensive lineman in the game. Up to 340 pounds, then 360, and then all the way to a peak of 392, Perry became known as The Refrigerator as he swatted away blockers and practically swallowed entire backfields. Even though he made most All-American teams, Perry still found many skeptics in the pro ranks. Sure, the man could make some fantastic plays, they pointed out, but you could never get a full game out of him. The burden of carrying all that weight around left him with no endurance, and Perry often sat out as many downs as he played.

One of those debating whether or not to draft Perry was Chicago Bear head coach Mike Ditka. Although he

Chicago coach Mike Ditka upset football tradition when he decided to give the ball to the biggest guy on the field.

had reservations about Perry's stamina, he finally concluded that he'd take a chance on him rather than have to try to figure out how to block him if he landed with someone else. So Chicago claimed Perry with their first-round choice in 1985.

Lengthy contract negotiations caused Perry to report to camp late that summer, and he certainly wasn't ready for what he found there. Perry had expected a quiet, learning year but instead found himself in the middle of a storm on his first day of camp. Poor, overweight William gasped and wheezed under the hot sun and finally had to drop out before practice was over. Bear defensive coordinator Buddy Ryan—who didn't care for rookies to begin with—fumed that Perry was "a waste of money and a wasted draft choice." Ryan made it clear he wanted Perry down to 280 pounds, but, even at that weight, he didn't expect him to help the team much.

The season started with The Refrigerator sitting in steam baths, jogging, and working out in the gym to get himself down to about 305 pounds. Gradually, he found more playing time as a tackle in the Bears' fearsome "46" defense. Although he showed signs of the great strength that could cave in an entire side of the line, Ryan sniffed that "he hasn't shown me anything."

Then an unsettled score with the San Francisco 49ers changed everything. The previous season, the 49ers had trounced the Bears, 23-0, in the NFL championship game and afterwards had snickered, "Next time bring an offense." One of the trick plays the 49ers had used involved placing 275-pound lineman Guy McIntyre in the backfield as a lead blocker on short yardage plays.

When the two teams met again on October 21, Ditka had his revenge plotted. First of all, his Bears took care of the score, manhandling the defending champs easily. Then came the personal touch. Ditka decided to go one up on the 49ers trick offense by using The Refrigerator. Perry laughed when told about the plan—and so did everyone else. Perry gained a few yards, the Bears had their fun, and everyone expected that to be the end of it.

But Ditka had accidently made an interesting discovery. "How do you stop a 305-pound battleship going full speed?" he wondered. Two weeks later, the answer came. You don't. Chicago turned The Refrigerator loose on three goal-line plays. On two occasions, he all but buried Green Bay Packer linebacker George Cumby in the artificial turf as Walter Payton scored easily. On the third play, Perry dove in himself for the score.

Immediately, the idea of the "whale

Perry's gap-toothed charm showed he was "just having fun."

block" rocked pro football. Other teams tried loading up their big guns around the goal line, but without much success. In a futile effort, the New York Jets tried Mark Gastineau and Joe Klecko, both All-Pro defensive linemen, in a backfield formation. But The Refrigerator was news. His innocent, fun-loving nature made him all the more enjoyable, and he took all kidding with a huge, gap-toothed grin. Perry was more than happy to add to the legend he was creating. He told of how he had to pour a whole box of cereal into a mixing bowl for his breakfast and of eating six chickens at a sitting. And he laughed along with jokes about how, rather that asking for a menu at a restaurant, he had to ask for an estimate. Before long, The Refrigerator was appearing in all kinds of commercials and was swamped with hundreds of offers he had to turn down.

While the Bears romped their way through their schedule, Ditka continued experimenting with his new national hero. The next time Chicago played the Packers, Perry came in for another offensive play and surprised Green Bay by slipping into the end zone to catch a touchdown pass. In a game against the Dallas Cowboys, The Refrigerator caused howls around the country with his exuberant blocking. Seeing that Walter Payton was being stopped just short of the goal line, Perry grabbed his fellow running back and tried to drag him into the end zone. Although it was illegal and cost the Bears a 10-yard penalty, the play added to The

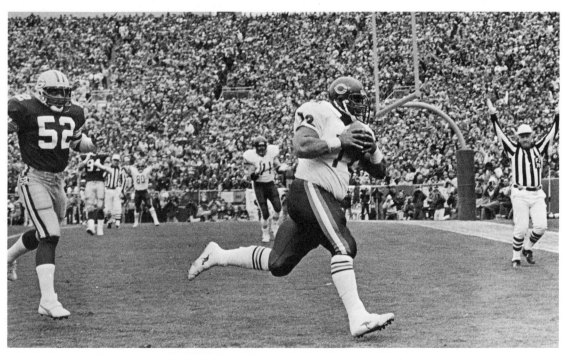

Not content with being pro football's largest running back, the athletic Perry turned pass receiver for this score to win a close game against the Packers.

Refrigerator's fame. Back on the ground against Atlanta, Perry lumbered through the Falcons for his third touchdown of the year.

Not everything was fun and games, however. Chicago kept a close watch on Perry's weight, and they held him to a diet program designed by a nutritionist. Perry, meanwhile, buckled down to the task of playing defense. While all that hoopla was fun, Perry said he'd rather have a sack than a touchdown. By the end of the year, Perry had become an explosive force in the Bears' famous defensive unit that dominated their opponents.

During the 1985 play-offs, Perry and his mates overwhelmed the New York Giants and the Los Angeles Rams with shutout performances. Thanks to the snarling Chicago defense, the Super Bowl contest against New England had about as much the suspense and tension as feeding time at the zoo. But thanks to The Refrigerator, the one-sided show wasn't totally boring. When he wasn't playing the Patriots' star guard John Hannah to a standstill, Perry was aiming his 308 pounds at the Patriot goal line. In the first half, he rolled to his right, intending to become the largest passer in football history, but he was sacked when his receiver failed to get open. Later, when the contest was no longer

in doubt, Perry gave one last demonstration of his powerful body's impact when he laid waste to the Patriots' right side and roared in from one yard out for a touchdown in Chicago's 46-10 victory.

With his weight swelling into the 330-pound range during 1986, Perry lost the quick start that he needed to play "whale back." But the extra weight did nothing to tarnish his reputation as The Refrigerator. Perry merely settled down to being a plain, old defensive tackle. With Perry overfilling the right tackle spot, the Bears' defense again mauled opponents. They took up the slack for a sputtering offense to help the Bears to a 14-2 mark before they fell to Washington in the play-offs.

As for William, his young career could best be summed up in his own words. "I was born big, and I ain't disappointing nobody."

WILLIAM PERRY: THE REFRIGERATOR

Born: 1962 in Aiken, South Carolina

Size: 6 feet, 2 inches; 300-340 pounds

College: Clemson University

Pro Draft: 1985; first round by Chicago Bears

All-Pro: none

Pro Bowl: none

Team Records:

YEAR	TEAM	WINS	LOSSES	TIES	POINTS	POINTS ALLOWED
1985	Chicago	15	1	0	456	198
1986	Chicago	14	2	0	352	187

First-Place Finishes: 1985, 1986

NFC Titles: 1985

Super Bowl Titles: 1985

ACKNOWLEDGMENTS: The photographs are reproduced through the courtesy of: pp. 1, 15, 31, 32, 40, 52, 56, 63, 70 (bottom), 72, 76, 77, Vernon J. Biever; pp. 2, 11, St. Louis Football Cardinals; pp. 6, 26, Pittsburgh Steelers; pp. 9, 19, 20, Pro Football Hall of Fame; p. 12 (left), Los Angeles Raiders; pp. 12 (right) (Denny Landwehr Babst Photographic Services), 61, 64, Cincinnati Bengals; p. 13, New England Patriots; pp. 14, 49, San Diego Chargers Football Club; pp. 16, 42, 43, Detroit Lions; pp. 22, 28, 46, 58, UPI/Bettmann Newsphotos; pp. 25, 34, 36, 55, Baltimore Colts; p. 38, New York Jets; p. 44, Los Angeles Rams; p. 48, Houston Oilers; p. 50, Kansas City Chiefs; p. 54, Michigan State University; p. 60, Ohio State University (Chance Brockway); pp. 66, 69, 70 (top), Washington Redskins; p. 74, Clemson University; p. 75, Chicago Bears. Front cover: Bill Smith. Back cover: Houston Oilers (top left), Baltimore Colts (bottom left), St. Louis Football Cardinals (right).